7 Steps to Finding & Living Your Passion

Your Guide to Happiness and Purpose

By Meri Har-Gil

Copyright Notice

The information contained in this report is strictly for educational purposes, and not every recommendation is right for everyone. Therefore, if you wish to apply ideas you read about, you are taking full responsibility for your actions. The author shall in no event be held liable to any party for any direct, indirect, punitive, special, incidental or other consequential damages arising directly or indirectly from any use of this material.

Contents

INTRODUCTION: YOUR JOURNEY STARTS HERE 5

RECIPE FOR HAPPINESS 9

HAPPINESS IS A CHOICE YOU MAKE 13

STEP 1 USING CURIOSITY & CREATIVITY 19

STEP 2 QUESTIONS TO FIND YOUR PASSION 27

STEP 3 PEAK EXPERIENCES AND EXISTING TALENTS 33

STEP 4 BARRIERS TO SUCCESS 37

STEP 5 GOAL SETTING 47

STEP 6 TURNING PASSION INTO REALITY 53

STEP 7 LIVING YOUR PASSION 59

CONCLUSION BE UNSTOPPABLE 67

APPENDIX 71

7 Steps to Finding & Living Your Passion

Introduction:

Your Journey Starts Here

Dear Reader, Thank you for your interest in this e-book. I'm thrilled that you want to find purpose and happiness in life, and I'm honoured to be part of your journey.

I know how important finding your passion is to personal fulfillment. It is a road that I walked myself, and now I live with more purpose and energy than I did when I was younger. Another thing I know: you and I are not alone. Many people are on a quest for a more meaningful life.

How do I know? Because - I talk to women every day, who express the desire to find and live their passions. Their stories fill the pages of this e-book.

As a life coach, I talk with many women who share this desire. They come from many different backgrounds, but they have one thing in common: they want more out of life. They aren't fulfilled in their current jobs or life situations. Changes must be made so they can live the lives they were meant to live. I help them make those changes, and I share many of my strategies throughout this e-book.

In addition to coaching, I also own and operate my own Spa. We all know that women love to talk during haircuts, pedicures and facials. Even in this setting, I often hear women express how frustrated they are with their lives and how they hope for something better.

I know how that feels because I felt it, too. I came to a point in my life where I knew I needed to make a change. While I loved managing a business, I knew my real passion was helping people. For this reason, I decided to become a life coach. The road has been long, but with hard work, accountability, and lots of positive thinking, I've succeeded! I know you can, too.

In the pages that follow, I'll share with you the strategies for success I've learned through my own personal journey, as well as, from others. I've broken the information down into seven steps. Take your time reading each chapter, and be true to yourself when you reflect.

Let's take the first step toward finding your passion together! Sincerely,

Meri Har-Gil

Recipe for Happiness

Audrey is unhappy in every sense of the word. She always looks on the negative side of things, and she dreads the start of each new day. She loathes her job, her family drives her crazy, and she's constantly complaining about some new ache or pain in her body. Audrey trudges through life like she has a 50-pound weight around her neck.

Lisa is a joyful, vibrant person. Even when things don't go her way, she manages to see the bright side. She looks forward to going to work and spending time with her family. She takes time to refresh and rejuvenate herself. She seems to skip energetically from one day to the next.

What is the difference between Audrey and Lisa? Why is one woman so happy and the other so unhappy? Is there something Lisa knows that Audrey doesn't?

The truth is happiness isn't based on circumstances or luck. There is no recipe that works for everyone. Happiness is a choice that each person makes. No matter what life hands you, it's possible to find contentment and peace.

The good news is you can make choices that can lead to a happier life. One of the most important choices is deciding to follow your passion. This means working hard doing what you love to do.

If you feel like your life is boring or stagnant, or you know you're not doing what you should be doing, then it's time to make a change. There may be obstacles or fears holding you back from accomplishing your goals, but you can get past them and make your dreams happen.

Some people aren't quite sure what their true passion is. They want to work toward being successful, but they aren't sure what it is that they can do. Finding your passion is possible, but it may take some soul-searching. Your passion might be right in front of you and you don't even realize it.

What's more, it is possible to make money by working toward your passion. You just need to see the moneymaking angle. Don't avoid your passion because you don't think it can financially sustain you, because, chances are, it can.

The purpose of this e-book is to help you find and live your passion. You will learn seven techniques that will help you identify your passion and strategies that will help you turn dreams into reality.

Reflect

Do you feel more like Audrey or Lisa right now in your life? Why?

Happiness Is a Choice You Make

Betty describes herself as a "perpetual malcontent." She says that she came out of the womb with a scowl. She doesn't even try to have a positive outlook because she believes she was born with a negative personality. "I'm just a naturally grumpy person," Betty hisses. "People just have to deal with it."

It's true that personality traits are influenced by genetics, but they aren't the sole determining factor of the way you view life. If you're not a happy person, you can change. Happiness is a choice you make each day as you face situations. You have full control over your life and your happiness.

There are many factors by which people measure happiness. Some people think money is happiness. Others will only be happy if they achieve education, status and honor. For others, happiness is as simple as a nice car. Unfortunately, true happiness is much more complex. Things can't create it; circumstances can't provide it.

Happiness is a choice.

Valerie is a highly respected executive with a mind-boggling salary. Everyone at the office respects her and defers to her judgment. She has a husband and two children, and they all look like they stepped out of the pages of a magazine. They live peacefully in an exclusive, manicured community. From the outside, Valerie has the perfect life.

If we remove the mask, we discover that Valerie is miserable. She's addicted to pain medication and has to excuse herself during corporate meetings to pop pills. Her playboy husband is hardly ever home, and neither is she, so she's a stranger to her two young kids, who throw tantrums to get her attention.

Remember, happiness isn't about external factors. It's about what's on the inside.

Happiness Is Subjective

What makes one person happy may not make another person happy. You might find happiness in seeking thrills like bungee jumping and skydiving. Someone with a fear of heights would consider your idea of "fun" torture.

Everyone seeks happiness in his or her own way. For most people, there is nothing wrong with the things that bring them joy. You may be told you're crazy, but that's okay. The choices you make for happiness are going to be different than someone else's because everyone is unique. Don't put aside what makes you happy because you're afraid of what other people will say.

Positive Choices for Happiness

While there is no checklist of choices that are guaranteed to bring everyone happiness, there are a few things that you can do to take care of your mind and body to promote a healthier and therefore happier lifestyle.

Sleep

You need sleep so that your body can function properly. When you don't get enough sleep, you're likely to be moody and irritable. You won't think as clearly or quickly. To get more sleep, you may need to change your daily schedule so you can get to bed earlier. You also might need to encourage other people in your household to help you more if you're working too hard or too late at night.

Exercise

Exercise produces endorphins in your body, which promote feelings of happiness. Exercise is important for total health, but this doesn't mean you need a heavy exercise routine to be happy. However, you should try to sweat everyday. It isn't about losing weight. It's about creating health and happiness.

Meditation

Practicing meditation doesn't mean you belong to a cult or a specific religion. Meditation is a time of quiet reflection and peace where you concentrate on restful, rejuvenating thoughts or empty your mind completely. Doctors have proven that meditation generates brain activity on the left side, which produces a positive emotion in the body.

Reflect

Do you consider yourself a naturally happy or unhappy person?

Do you need more sleep, exercise or quiet time in your day to promote happiness? How can you make that happen?

Step 1

Using Curiosity & Creativity

Rose's life is monotonous. She wakes up, goes to work, comes home, sleeps and starts over again. She eats the same meals each week, wears the same clothes, watches the same TV shows. Her life is predictable. While she does find comfort in routine, the same things day in and day out are starting to irritate her. Rose wants something more, but she's too comfortable to reach for it.

Have you ever felt like Rose? You've hit a groove, and life is fairly stable, not throwing you many curveballs. While it's nice to feel at ease, sometimes an unyielding routine can stifle a person's growth.

When we get too comfortable, we're sometimes reluctant to try new things or seek out new experiences. We become complacent and bored with life. When we get to this point, we ask ourselves, "What happened to my passion and energy?"

It's difficult to rediscover your passions if your life doesn't hold any excitement or variety. One way to add excitement to your life is to develop your curiosity and creativity. By sparking curiosity and creativity, you begin your journey toward finding your passion.

Building Curiosity

Some people are naturally inquisitive. They're full of questions. Others naturally accept things the way they are. If you aren't naturally curious, here are a few ways to cultivate your curiosity.

Ask Questions

Train yourself to think critically about things. When you don't understand something, ask someone to explain it to you. Go beyond surface questions and try to understand the root of the issue. It's not about being skeptical or negative. It's about trying to gain a full, round picture of something, whether it is a person, thing or idea.

Some people don't like to ask questions because they think it makes them look unintelligent. On the contrary, asking thoughtful questions can make you look smarter in most situations. Plus, nobody likes a know-it-all. Humbling yourself enough to ask a question enables you to stand stronger in the end.

Don't Take Things for Granted

When building curiosity, don't accept things at face value. If something doesn't seem right, find out why. If your boss, child or spouse is sensitive about something, don't just accept that as part of his or her personality. Ask why this particular issue is difficult for them. If there is a rule or law that seems unfair, discover its purpose and evaluate its effectiveness. Digging deeper, you'll likely unearth many interesting truths.

Keep an Open Mind

A curious person doesn't close his or her mind to different possibilities, even if they sound crazy. A curious person tries to imagine what life would look like under different circumstances. This allows you to look beyond what life currently offers and grasp at new possibilities.

When you're set in your ways, it's difficult to see things from another perspective. Your mind isn't willing to accept other angles. This can hinder you in several ways:

First, if you can't imagine your life taking a new, more exciting and vibrant path, then you probably won't have much motivation to take action on this passion.

Second, you may reject viable ideas as impossible because you can't imagine succeeding. You haven't prepared your mind to be open to new possibilities; therefore, you may miss out on important opportunities.

Don't Label Something as Boring

Curious people are willing to try new things, because they wonder what it will be like. This isn't about seeking thrills; it's about being open to new experiences. If someone asks you to try a new activity, travel to a new place or eat a new kind of food, accept the challenge, even if it doesn't sound like much fun. By opening the door to new things, you add spice to your life and you may even discover your passion.

Be a Lifelong Learner

When was the last time you learned something new? Curious people are constantly learning things, because they ask questions and are genuinely interested in the answers. Think of new knowledge as little jewels. Every time you learn a new fact, you add a precious jewel to your collection.

People commonly say they're too old to learn new things. This isn't true. Take a course at a community college or through your city. Join a book club and read things you wouldn't normally choose. Learn a new sport and then join a local league.

Some people associate learning with school. If school wasn't a fun experience for you, you may shy away from learning new things. Remember, not all learning happens in a classroom. Also, keep your long-term goals in mind when you're learning something new; this will remind you of why you're going through the trouble. Whatever you do, don't think of it as a burden. Instead, recognize it as a privilege, and it will add excitement to your life.

Building Creativity

Many people associate creativity with artistic ability. You don't need to learn how to paint like Van Gogh to be a creative person. Simply put, creativity is making something new and fresh. For example, a creative mom might get her kids involved with preparing dinner rather than just serving them in front of the TV. Voila! Her kids get cooking lessons from mom each week: that's something that wasn't there before.

Here are some ways you can add more creativity to your daily life.

Make It a Game

Yes, a game! Give yourself a mission to accomplish and a set of rules. Then work within those rules to reach your goal. You can do this in any setting. For example, your mission is to be more sociable at work. The rules are you have to talk with at least one person per hour and three new people per day. Or maybe your goal is to simply fold laundry. The rule is that you can't fold an item the same way twice. Even if it seems trivial, it will make your day more fun and sharpen your mind.

Express Yourself

Creative people love to customize! They enjoy taking what's blah and making it brilliant. They do this by asking themselves, "How do I want this to be?" They look at is as a way to express themselves.

Expressing yourself can be shown in the way you display dinner on the plate. You might choose to dress up a meal with fancy garnishes. You may change the way you do a presentation at work and completely alter the style from the way everyone else does it. View every activity as a way to express yourself creatively.

The Payoff

When you cultivate curiosity and creativity in yourself, life will go from black-and-white to colour. You'll start to see the beauty in the things around you. You'll have more drive and energy to grow and develop as a person. You'll be ready to find your passion.

Reflect

What is one specific way you can be more curious?

What is one specific way you can be more creative?

(Don't give a general answer like, "Read something every day." Think of something specific like, "Read one biography each month" or "Read X's blog everyday.")

Step 2

Questions to Find Your Passion

Dina always knew she wanted to be a chef. She loved helping her mother in the kitchen when she was a child. She's always appreciated the flavors and textures of food. She always knew that preparing and serving food was what she wanted to do with her life.

Not all of us are like Dina. She found her passion early in life and stuck to it. Maybe you had childhood dreams, but you put them away when it came time to select a "real" career. Or maybe you always lived your life for others and never had time to consider what you wanted.

Now, it's time to find your passion!

By carefully answering the questions that follow, you will understand more about yourself and what makes you most happy. Use the worksheet in the appendix at the end of this e-book to record your own responses and feelings as you read through this chapter.

Also, be completely honest when responding. Don't think of only the "safe" answers. Don't worry about anyone ridiculing you. If you aren't honest, you're only hindering your own progress and success.

What really inspires and engages you?

This is ultimately what you need to know to find your passion. If you're passionate about something, that means it inspires your soul and stimulates your mind. What are the types of things you find engaging and exciting? What do you love to do? What are you doing when you feel most alive?

If you couldn't fail, what would you do?

Many people don't do things because they're afraid to fail, or maybe they've failed in the past. If there is something that you would definitely do if you knew there wasn't a chance whatsoever of failing, what would that be?

If you were forced to start over again, what would you do?

Imagine having a clean slate, a fresh start at life. Envision yourself going back in time or losing everything that is currently tying you down. If you started over again, would you take advantage of the new beginning or would you make the same choices that led to where you are today?

If money weren't an issue, what would you do?

Many people have dreams they wish to pursue but they never attempt them because they can't afford to get started. What would you love to do if you had the money to do it? This doesn't necessarily have to be related to starting a business. If you were independently wealthy and didn't have to work, what would you do with your time?

What is your biggest dream?

If you have a big dream, what is it? Is there something you really want to do that you daydream about? Maybe you fantasize about quitting your job as a mechanic and racing cars. When you fantasize about a better life, what does that life look like?

What passion are you afraid of owning or admitting to?

Many people have hobbies they are afraid to talk about out of fear of being ridiculed by other people.

Maybe you tried sharing it with someone and were told it was a silly dream. Chances are there are other people like you who have the same hobbies and passions.

As a child, what did you really want to be?

Did you have dreams as a child that didn't turn out quite as expected? Do you still wonder what it would have been like if you followed your childhood dreams? If you had the opportunity, would you follow this dream today?

If you were going to die in the near future, what would you regret not doing?

They say hindsight is 20/20. People on deathbeds have said they would've lived their lives differently if given the chance. If a doctor told you that you only had a few weeks left, what would your regrets be? What would you want to do before your time was up?

What does your home say about you?

Your true passion may be sitting right in front of you on your bookshelf or staring at you from your walls. You may have collections of items, such as magazines, that speak to your interests. You may dedicate a room in your house to a weekend hobby. Take a look around your home and see if some of the decorations are a clue to what your true passion is.

What is the biggest barrier stopping you from following your dream?

Name all of the things that have caused you to not follow your big dream. These things can include people who don't support you, lack of money, and nagging fears. Many of these barriers can be overcome. We'll talk more about barriers in step four.

Now that you've answered these questions, you should have a good idea of some of the things that could possibly make you happy. The goal of this chapter is to understand what you enjoy most, what you were made to do. This is your passion.

Reflect

Use the worksheet in the appendix to respond to each of the questions in this chapter.

After doing this, ask yourself, "Do I have a better idea of what my passion might be?"

Step 3

Peak Experiences and Existing Talents

Another way to find your passion is to look back on past life experiences. Two things to focus on are peak experiences and existing talents. These confidence-building memories can direct you toward your passion.

Peak Experiences

Your peak experiences are times in your life where you excelled. These experiences may be on your list of "best days." Consider your accomplishments, whether they're work-related or personal. Maybe you've received awards for a job well done or worked hard to accomplish a long-term goal. Think about times when your heart swelled with pride and gratitude, and you knew you did the right thing at the right time.

A peak experience doesn't have to involve your professional skills. Receiving an award for salesperson of the year or getting a big promotion certainly qualify as peak experiences, but so does cooking an excellent meal for a large group of people or hand making an exquisite gift for a friend.

Not all peak experiences happen in rooms full of applauding people. Some peak experiences are personal, and only you know about them. Maybe one of your peak experiences was when you convinced your best friend to tell her parents she was bulimic. Even though it was difficult, you felt purposeful and invigorated when you helped your friend work through a crisis.

Existing Talents

Existing talents are skills you have. What are you good at? Are you good at organizing or marketing? You might be good at something you don't even realize, such as public speaking, making phone calls, baking, or gardening. Sometimes we say, "Oh, that's not a real skill," because the talent comes so easily. Yes, it is definitely a real skill.

You don't have to be an expert to consider yourself talented. Chances are, you're knowledgeable about a hobby you enjoy. You read about it and are familiar with little-known facts. Think about something you are very knowledgeable about because you choose to be, not because you are required to be at work. Even though you aren't a recognized expert in the field, you still know more than the average person.

Think about talents that you used to have that are now a little rusty. For example, maybe you used to be an avid runner, and always wanted to win the New York City Marathon. But now you're a smoker and you wrote that dream off years ago. That doesn't mean you can't get back into shape and go for your big dream.

Reflect

Use the worksheet in the appendix to make a list of your peak experiences and existing talents.

After doing this, do you now know what your passion is?

Step 4

Barriers to Success

Congratulations! You've identified your passion. You know what you love, and you wish you could dedicate the rest of your life to it É but you can't.

There are too many obstacles in your path. You know if you start you'll fail. So, why try? What's the point?

Let's banish this kind of thinking right now!

Yes, there may be challenges ahead if you want to live your dream, but you can overcome them. Don't give up before you've even started just because the road seems rough. You will persevere, and the victory will be all the more sweet when you look back on how far you've come.

Keep the big picture in mind throughout this chapter, as we look in detail at some common barriers to success.

People

"That's the stupidest idea I've ever heard!" "You? Do that? Fat chance!" "Are you sure this is what you want?" Sometimes it takes only one negative comment to deflate you completely. If someone ridicules your idea, it makes you feel foolish, one of the worst feelings in the world. The fact is, you may feel foolish at times. It's okay. Remember, geniuses have been made fun of for their desire to do the impossible.

First, realize that your desire to live out your passion isn't going to please everyone in your life. The most important thing is that you're doing what you were meant to do. Don't worry about what other people think of you.

Having said that, it's also important to take care of the people that depend on you. If you're quitting your job to be a painter, but you have five kids at home who depend on your paycheck, this is not a wise decision. If your family is unhappy, you won't be happy even if you are doing what you love.

Second, surround yourself with supportive people. Don't seek the company of people who berate and belittle you. They'll only discourage you. Instead, seek out like-minded individuals who share your passion. Together, work toward your goals and keep each other accountable.

Having said that, don't surround yourself with yes-men (people who support you even if you're wrong). Make sure that the people in your life love you enough to encourage you but also tell you the truth, even if it hurts.

When you have the right support, you can do anything.

Money

Gina is by far the best florist at the flower shop where she works. Customers specifically ask for her to design their bouquets, because of her creativity and attention to detail. Her dream is to start her own shop, but she knows that she'll never be able to save enough money for startup costs.

Let's face it, some passions cost money - lot of money. While this is a very real barrier for many people, it can be overcome.

First, consider low-cost alternatives. For example, if you love making aromatherapy candles and want to open your own shop, consider selling online and in your home first. You may find that digital profits are much higher than they would be at a brick-and-mortar store. This first step may provide you with the funds you need to open the store in the future.

Another option is to cut personal costs and raise money. While this is a sacrifice, it's worth it if it means that you're closer to achieving your passion. Cut costs by removing extraneous expenses from your budget. Work your passion into your monthly budget, figuring out where you can cut back to make room for it. Raise money by selling things you don't need or working an extra job. This may seem drastic, but when you really want to achieve your dream, you're willing to do just about anything.

Work your passion into your savings plan. Don't blow the money you save on something else. Put it in a special bank account and don't touch it until you're ready.

Money is one of the most common excuses people give for why they can't live their dreams. Don't fall into this trap. While it may mean sacrifice in the short-term, it will pay big rewards in the long run.

Time

Sarah wants to become a scuba-diving instructor, but she can't ever find time to take the certification course. She works 10-hour days with a 1-hour commute each way. When she factors in her personal life, this leaves her zero time to pursue her goal.

Time is another reason many people procrastinate making their dreams a reality. If you're a slave to your job and don't even have time for family, you may feel selfish taking time out for yourself to pursue a personal passion. Don't feel guilty. With some rearranging, you can make the time you need.

First, you must realize that you can't find time. You must make time. This means you need to cut back on something in order to put time toward your passion. Yes, you must make a sacrifice. Consider waking up an hour or two earlier every day or staying up a little bit later. Just remember that sleep is also important for happiness.

If you get a 1-hour lunch break, bring your hobby to work with you. This way, you can work on your passion an hour each day, and it may give you something to look forward to if you consider work a bore. If you have a long commute, think about taking public transportation. On the ride, you can work on your laptop or read a book to learn more about your passion. If you drive a lot, listen to audio books that teach about your passion.

It's also common for people to say they have no time when they really do. If you spend a few hours every week watching television or surfing the internet, you can use that time to work on your passion instead.

You may think, "Just an hour a day isn't much. I'll never realize my dream if I work so little on it." Remember, any progress is better than none. In step five, we'll talk about goal setting. If you can break your goals down into small pieces, you can accomplish a little piece each day, bringing you closer and closer to realizing your big dream.

Job

If your current job is the reason you cannot live out your passion, it's probably a time issue. People spend most of their day at work. If you're not doing what you love, this can seem like wasted time. If you're considering quitting or changing jobs to pursue your passion, you need to consider it carefully.

First, are you a slave to your employer? If you're working very long hours with no hope for promotion or development or relief, you may want to consider getting a new job. Everyone should have some time for themselves and opportunities to grow.

Second, do you dread going to work? If so, think about switching jobs. You're obviously not living your passion at work, and if you don't enjoy what you do, you won't ever be truly successful at it.

If you've determined that you need to switch jobs, try getting a job that is related to your passion. If you're currently working as an administrative assistant at an advertising agency, but your real passion is humanitarian work, try getting a job as an administrative assistant at a non-profit. That way, you can learn more about the field each day at work. Don't worry about getting the perfect job. Just try for something that will allow you to develop in the right areas.

Don't quit your job or take a lower-paying job if it means your family will suffer. If you can't support your spouse or kids, you won't be happy. They may come to resent your passion because it has brought hardship to your household. Remember to care and love those who have been entrusted to you first. This is the right thing to do, and if you do it, opportunities will open for you to pursue your dreams.

Fears

Nancy wants to start a travel blog, but she's afraid to write her first post. What if people hate it? What if nobody reads it? She's also afraid to tell her husband about it. What if he makes fun of her? Even scarier, what if she succeeds and her blog grows and she doesn't know how to handle it and she misses out on crucial opportunities or people steal her good ideas? Her head hurts, and she hasn't even begun.

Fear is something that you can and must overcome if you want to move forward. For being an intangible feeling, fear can immobilize people for years.

For many, their biggest fear is the fear of failure. This is perfectly natural when starting something new. Not many people are immediately successful. Most people experience failures along the way. One way to lessen the fear of failure is to think about how you will respond to potential challenges before they happen. If you have an idea of how to troubleshoot problems, you won't be as afraid of encountering them.

Another idea is to change the way you think about failure. If you look at a failure as a learning experience, it doesn't seem so ominous. Knowing that you'll grow from your mistakes, turning negatives into positives, will help you press forward.

Some people even have a fear of success. Have you ever known someone who saved their money for something and as soon as they saved a substantial amount, they blew it on something they didn't need?

Later they kicked themselves and began the saving process all over again.

The fear to succeed is also natural. Some people have a low self-image, and they don't believe themselves good enough or capable of being successful. Others are afraid they won't be able to handle things if their idea succeeds. One way to overcome this is to make a growth plan for your idea. What kind of challenges will you face if your dream succeeds? How will you deal with those challenges? If you know what you'll do ahead of time, facing these situations won't seem as frightening.

Lack of Knowledge

Jodi is thinking about quitting her menial job at the newspaper to become a freelance writer, but she's only ever worked in newspapers. She's not sure how to get work as a freelancer. She doesn't know how to pay or get paid or how to protect herself from getting cheated. There are so many questions and so few answers, so she just sits at her desk day after day wishing she could be her own boss.

Thankfully, a lack of knowledge is one of the easiest barriers to overcome. The only challenge is obtaining the knowledge you need.

For some people, this may just mean reading books or browsing the Internet to gain more understanding. Others may need to take classes or get a new degree or certification. However much time you'll need to invest in learning, break it down into small goals: read one article per day, take one class per semester. You'll be happy knowing that you're progressing toward a fulfilling reward instead of doing nothing.

It's Possible!

So many people look at these barriers and think to themselves, it's impossible! Well, it is possible.

Yes, there are challenges to work through, but don't use them as an excuse or be victimized by your circumstances. There are things in your control. You can control the barriers in your life and in your mind. You can find ways to creatively overcome these challenges so you can get started living your passion. Stand up and say "No!" to barriers that are in your way and start living your dreams.

Reflect

Use the worksheet in the appendix to identify the specific barriers in your life and ways to overcome them.

After doing this, do you feel like you can start living your passion now? If not, why? When may you be able to start in the future?

Step 5

Goal Setting

Teresa's big dream is to run for city council. It's something she's always wanted to do and she talks about it often. Every year around elections, she says that it'll be her name on the ballot next time. Teresa knows what she needs to do to run for city council, but she never seems to get started early enough. One year she told family and friends that she was running; she even handed out buttons. That's the last they heard about it.

Obviously, Teresa has no follow-through. If you're going to achieve your goal and live your passion, you have to be practical about it. While it's good to keep the big picture in mind, you can't just talk in vague terms about how you're going to do something someday.

To get anything done, you have to set goals and achieve them.

Why Set Goals?

Goal setting may seem a little too structured for you if you're a free spirit. However, it's important for several reasons. It forces you to break down large, complex tasks into manageable pieces. You can see forward progress (or lack of progress) and keep yourself on track so you don't get distracted or procrastinate.

Goal setting takes a "someday" concept and grounds it in everyday life. You can actually see how close you're getting to reaching your dream. It can be very empowering and inspiring.

Break It Down

What does a goal look like? First, there are overall goals. This is the big-picture goal you want to achieve. Examples of overall goals are starting a business, finishing school, learning to cook, moving to a foreign country. Overall goals are complex and multi-faceted.

Overall goals can be broken down into smaller goals called milestones. If your goal is to create a profitable craft blog, perhaps some milestone goals include designing the website, marketing the website, designing 5 new craft items to sell and writing 10 initial blog posts.

Each milestone goal can be broken down into specific tasks. Tasks are easy and quick to accomplish, usually involving just a few simple actions. For example, marketing the craft blog can be broken down into tasks, such as starting a Facebook page and Twitter account and signing up to join similar blogs.

What about your big idea? What are the milestones and tasks needed to accomplish it? Use the chart in the appendix to brainstorm and track your goals. Keep the chart where you can see it. If you stuff it in a drawer or in a file cabinet, you'll forget about it.

Assign a Date

That's right. After you've broken down your big goal, you need to assign dates to each milestone and task. If you work toward a completion date, you're more likely to actually get things done, rather than saying, "I plan to do it eventually." A date makes the goal more real.

When you assign dates, be strict with yourself, but don't stress yourself out. If you don't take your deadlines seriously, then there's no point in using them. But don't drive yourself insane trying to meet a deadline that isn't realistic. If you find that a particular task is going to take longer than you thought, adjust the dates accordingly.

Commit to Yourself

If you're really serious about accomplishing a big goal, you may want to write up an official contract from yourself to yourself, or use the sample contract in the appendix. Sign and date it, committing to following your goal-setting chart as well as you possibly can.

If you break your contract, you're breaking your commitment to yourself. You have only yourself to answer to and you have only yourself to blame. If you're tempted to blow off a deadline, ask, "Am I willing to break my promise to myself?"

Reward Yourself

Some of your milestone goals may take months, even years to complete. When you reach a goal, throw a little party for yourself. Do something special or out-of-the-norm. Buy a bottle of wine. Schedule a massage. Nab a new pair of shoes. Go camping for the weekend. Get your friends together for a chocolate party.

Reflect

Use the chart in the Appendix to brainstorm and set goals for the future.

After doing this, ask yourself, "How do I feel about my goals and my passion now that I've done this?"

Step 6

Turning Passion into Reality

You've identified your passion and your big dream. You've thought through the challenges, and you've set goals for accomplishing your dream.

BUT - How do you take that first step?

Here are some lifestyle tips that will help you when you're on the brink of plunging headfirst into your passion. They will help you incorporate your passion into your everyday life.

Believe You Can

One of the most important things for success is believing that you will succeed. If you don't believe it's possible, then you're not ready to start until you do. Relax and visualize yourself on your favorite talk show gushing about your success. You should feel empowered when you think about your endeavor, not defeated.

Keep Your Spirits Up

Your attitude can make you or break you. You need to maintain a positive perspective. This is a choice you make. Don't let the little things discourage or upset you. Even when things get difficult, remind yourself, "I'm living my passion right now. This is what I've always wanted to do. I knew there would be challenges, but I'll work through them." If you're constantly thinking negatively, you're more likely to throw in the towel.

Hone Your Idea

As you take the first steps toward your big idea, you may realize that you need to tweak it a little. As you gain more knowledge and experience, you may find better ways of doing things. Take your idea and make it better by chiseling away at the details. Don't be afraid to change your idea. Things evolve over time.

This is an especially good activity to do when you're in a waiting period. If you're waiting on something outside of your control, such as test results or building permits, use that time to hone your idea.

Build Momentum

The opposite of momentum is procrastination. You have your goals laid out, so act on them! Act right away. Don't sit around waiting for the perfect time to start.

The same principle applies to a problem you need to fix. You need to act on it. The more responsive you are and the less wait-time you allow yourself, then the more momentum will increase. You'll see results quicker, which will make you want to take more action. You'll become more productive than you thought possible.

Make the Best of Your Resources

The creativity you learned about and cultivated in step one will come in handy at this time. You may not have the money or resources you need. That's when it's time to get creative. If you're a writer without a computer, go to the public library and use a free one. If you need childcare so you can have a few hours to work alone, ask a friend to watch your kids, and you watch hers in exchange.

If you can stretch what you have and reduce waste (of time, money and materials) then you'll be off to a great start.

Sacrifice and Hard Work

If you're hoping to be an overnight success, let's pop that balloon right now. Chances are, you won't be instantly successful. Attaining your dream will take hard work and sacrifice. That's why it's so important to find your passion something that's worth it for you.

There is no substitute for hard work. You may run across someone selling a scheme that promises a quick payoff. If it sounds too good to be true, it probably is. Only you can reach the goals you set for yourself. Embrace the long hours, because they will be rewarding in the end. Your achievement will mean something significant because it's the product of your own elbow grease, not some gimmick or shortcut.

Organize Your Life

Structure your life so that it includes time for your passion. For example, wake up early in the morning, brew coffee, read the paper, post on your blog, and update your Facebook page. Structuring your day so that it includes time for you to tackle one of your small tasks will make you feel like you're in control of your journey toward success.

Reflect

Are you ready to take the first step toward your passion right now? If not, make a list of what's holding you back.

Step 7

Living Your Passion

Patty took the plunge. After 20 years of working for other people, she finally started her own beauty salon. She thought it through, set her goals, saved the money, recruited quality employees, promoted her business, closed her eyes and jumped! Now she's got to swim.

Once you've made the decision to live your passion, how do you maintain it once you've started?

Here are a few key points to keep in mind as you begin to live your dream.

Stay Passionate

Before she opened her own salon, Patty thought it would be terrific being her own boss, but she didn't realize how much work it would be. She works twice as hard now than she did before. It'll be a few years before she's making as much money as she was before.

If you're in Patty's situation, it's easy to let your passion wane. Don't suffer from "the grass is greener" syndrome. This means that when you weren't living your passion, you wished you were. Now that you are living your passion, you wish things were back to normal. The grass is not always greener on the other side of the fence.

Keep in perspective the fact that you're living your dream. Even if you're working harder, your working at something you love, not a dreary job you could care less about. Enjoy the experience with all the ups and downs. Don't be fake, saying everything is great when it isn't. Be honest with yourself about your journey and let that fuel your passion. Remember, you're doing something you can be proud of, something fulfilling.

Stay Active

Just because she started her salon doesn't mean Patty is no longer tempted to procrastinate. Her list of goals is still a mile long, and there are times when she just doesn't feel like working on those tasks.

It's easy to loose momentum after you take the first step toward living your dream. This is especially true if you choose to pursue your dream part-time. If you're doing a little here and a little there, making inchworm progress, it's easy to convince yourself, "Oh, I'll just slack off for a couple of weeks. No big deal." Sometimes those two weeks can turn into two months or even two years.

Remember to keep your list of goals where you can see it. Enter your deadlines in your calendar or phone. Put up a sign that says "Action!" to remind yourself that the only way you'll progress toward your passion is through action.

You want also to have people on your team that are action-oriented. If you have a really supportive aunt that likes to sit around and talk but does not work hard, then you can't let her distract you while you work. Instead, she may be the right person to create hype for your endeavor. Make sure that the people in action-oriented roles are action-oriented people.

Always reward action. Never let goal setting go without some kind of reward. You want to reward everyone helping you Êand yourself. This doesn't mean you need to spend money you don't have. You can reward someone by writing a heartfelt thank-you card.

Don't Let Setbacks Stop You

The opening week of Patty's salon didn't go as well as she'd hoped. She didn't attract enough customers to offset her marketing and publicity expenses. She was really disappointed and was wondering if this is a sign that she should give up.

Reaching your goals will take hard work and things won't always go as planned. At times, you may burst into tears and want to throw in the towel. Success is never easy. Would you much rather be working hard toward something you care about, rather than toward an unfulfilling and dull career? This passion is yours and you own it, good and bad.

Look at setbacks as learning experiences. Recognize that it's all part of your on-the-job training. One day when you're helping someone else get started, you'll say to them, "Oh, yes. I made that mistake, too. I survived and so will you."

Continuous Improvement

After a few months, Patty's salon grew and she finally made a profit. "Ahhh," she thought, "Now I can put this thing on cruise control."

Not quite. If you want to sustain your passion long-term, you have to dedicate yourself to continuous improvement. Evaluate processes that are slowing you down, causing poor quality, or frustrating you. Always look for ways to innovate and stay at the top of your game.

Continuous improvement will not only better your business, it will invigorate you personally and help you not to lose energy or momentum. You'll feel like you're always striving to make things better, which means you always have a mission to accomplish. As you build curiosity and creativity, your mind will constantly look for innovative ways to do things differently. This will keep you from feeling ho-hum about your passion.

Model Your Heroes

Choose a handful (about five) people who share your passion and who you admire. These are people, who have done what you want to do and have been successful. Learn everything you can about them. How did they become successful? What did it take for them? If possible, contact them and ask the secrets to their success.

After you've learned about your heroes, model them. There's nothing wrong with following in the footsteps of those, who have gone before you. Don't blindly copy them, but make use of the same strategies that gave them good results. These may be business strategies, creative-thinking strategies or simply positive attitudes.

Measure Success Accurately

There is no one, universal measure of success. What does success mean to you personally?

For Patty, success doesn't mean becoming a millionaire and buying a new house or a fancy car. For her, success is having the freedom to make her own schedule and hire, who she wants to work with. Before she started her own salon, she craved a better work environment. Now that she owns her own salon, she can create the atmosphere she wants. To her, this is success, not necessarily making loads of cash.

The important thing is that you can look back on your life and know you did everything you wanted to do. No regrets. You won't say, "Oh, if only I'd been brave and done that." This is also a measure of success. Don't feel bad because you haven't increased your standard of living. Instead, be happy, because you've improved your quality of life.

Reflect

When it comes to living your passion, do you have rose-colored glasses on? Are you prepared for the realities of living your dream, including hard work?

Who are a few of your heroes? Why? What have they done to be successful?

What is your personal definition of success? At what point will you be content with living your dream?

Conclusion

Be Unstoppable

Dear Reader,

I want you to think of your passion. Now imagine someone living that passion everyday. Now imagine that person is you.

It can be. You've learned how to have the right attitude for success:

- ❖ Happiness is different for everyone. Don't stifle your passion just because it's uncommon or different.

- ❖ Happiness is a choice you make. If you choose to be unhappy, then living your passion won't be enough.

You've also learned the seven steps for finding and living your passion:

1. Cultivate a curious and creative mind to break out of your comfort zone.//
2. Ask yourself questions to discover what inspires you.
3. Use peak experiences and existing talents to pinpoint your passion.
4. Eliminate barriers to success.
5. Set specific and realistic goals to get started.
6. Take the first step with the right attitude.
7. Maintain your success with effective strategies.

A passion is something that you want and were meant to do with your life. You can live your passion if you choose to work hard and persevere. Remember, there is no recipe for instant success, but these steps provide you with guidance for how you can slowly and surely transform your life.

The only person, who can truly hinder you, is yourself. In order to progress toward your passion, you need to be unstoppable. That means you don't let roadblocks, whether external or internal, get in your way. Keep following the steps and watch how things change for the better.

There's one thing for certain: you're worth it.

I've seen too many women never have the courage to start down this road. I've seen many more take a few steps and then give up. I know that you can succeed if you keep at it. If I can do it, you can do it.

I also know that it's hard to do this alone. If you need support, consider connecting with a life coach like me. It's my job to help people work through obstacles to achieve a goal. I do it everyday it's my passion. I won't be your psychologist, your counselor or your mother. Instead, I will be your accountability partner, your cheerleader and your guide. Together, we'll create an active partnership that will propel you toward your dreams.

Schedule a FREE 20-Minute Coaching Session!

Contact me to schedule a free 20-minute coaching session, where we will discuss your goals and how I can help you achieve them. Free sessions are confidential and obligation-free with no strings attached. I'd love to meet you! If you would like to book a FREE strategy session simply go to my website - www.merihargil.com and start your journey today!.

Sincerely,

Meri Har-Gil

Appendix

Worksheet: Questions to Find Your Passion

Question	Your Response
What really inspires and engages you?	
If you couldn't fail, what would you do?	
If you were forced to start over again, what would you do?	
If money weren't an issue, what would you do?	

Question	Your Response
What is your biggest dream?	
What passion are you afraid of owning or admitting to?	
As a child, what did you really want to be?	
If you were going to die in the near future, what would you regret not doing?	
What does your home say about you?	
What is the biggest barrier stopping you from following your dream?	

Worksheet: Peak Experiences & Existing Talents

	Peak Experiences	Existing Talents
At work		
At home / with family and friends		
With hobbies		
Personal		

Make a list of your top 5 best days or best moments:

1. _____
2. _____
3. _____
4. _____
5. _____

Worksheet: Barriers to Success

Barrier	Solution
People	Who in your life is critical of your passion or affects you negatively? Who in your life is supportive and helpful?
Money	What ways can you cut startup costs? How can you make money to help with startup costs? How will you save this money?
Time	What can you cut out of your schedule to make time for your passion? Can you make time? (Ex: riding the bus to work)

Barrier	Solution
Job	Do you need to quit or switch jobs? Can you look for a job related to your passion?
Fears	What setbacks will you face? How can you overcome them? If you succeed, what will be the challenges? How will you handle them?
Lack of Knowledge	What do you still need to learn before you can start living your passion? How will you learn it?

Goal Setting Chart

Overall Goal: Deadline: Reward:		
Milestone: Deadline: Reward:	Task:	Deadline:
	Task:	Deadline:
	Task:	Deadline:
Milestone: Deadline: Reward:	Task:	Deadline:
	Task:	Deadline:
	Task:	Deadline:
Milestone: Deadline: Reward:	Task:	Deadline:
	Task:	Deadline:
	Task:	Deadline:
Milestone: Deadline: Reward:	Task:	Deadline:
	Task:	Deadline:
	Task:	Deadline:

7 Steps to Finding & Living Your Passion

Personal Contract

I, _____, enter into this agreement with myself that I will pursue the following goal to the best of my ability:

Description of goal:

I promise to

- Work toward this goal on a weekly basis
- Meet all the deadlines I assign to myself, within reason
- Refine, hone and improve this goal continually
- Acquire any skills necessary to reach this goal

I understand that if I break this contract, I will be hindering my own success and progress. I will let myself down. That is why I agree to put forth my best effort.

_____ _____

Signature   Date

CPSIA information can be obtained
at www.ICGtesting.com
Printed in the USA
LVHW070922160820
663324LV00016B/2467